In *The Truth Is* Avery M. Guess ensnares her reader in a terrifying drama of intimacy's invasions—incest, abuse, institutionalization, suicide, illness—that the reader, like the speaker, cannot escape. And yet, all the while, here too is the grace and salvation only the natural world offers us; here too is the guardian strength of ginkgo trees, thunderstorms, the Everglades, the ocean, the Miami sun. Here too is a whole woman's body, which, once she discovers she is never separate from the loving silence on which this good earth turns, becomes something so much greater than what she endures. And so do we.
—Rebecca Gayle Howell, author of *American Purgatory* and
   Render: An Apocalypse

Avery Guess's debut collection of poems *The Truth Is* is a brave document of survivorhood. The poems bear witness to childhood domestic & sexual violence, and ask the reader to listen with compassion, love, and tenderness. Formally varied, at turns, spare, narrative, and fantastical, the poems move with agility through possibility while refusing easy answers. Guess's book offers a necessary testimony for our times.
—Cathy Linh Che, Author of *Split*

It is impossible to read the poems in this collection without taking a breath after each one, calculating everything at stake. *The Truth Is* dismantles our tidy narratives—its poems thrash with honesty, renouncing shame while demanding we, as readers, help carry the load. It challenges us to put more effort into the terms: *witness, survivor, risk,* and *reckoning.*
—Rachel McKibbens, Author of *blud, Into the Dark & Emptying*
   Field, and Pink Elephant

The Truth Is

Avery M. Guess

Black
Lawrence
Press

www.blacklawrence.com

Executive Editor: Diane Goettel
Book Design: Amy Freels
Cover Design: Zoe Norvell

Copyright © 2019 Avery M. Guess
ISBN: 978-1-62557-711-5

Published 2019 by Black Lawrence Press.
Printed in the United States.

Contents

To Cathy and David, with all my love.

The Secret Swallower Reveals Her Swords

Imagine the first time someone looked at a sword and thought, *hey, I'd like to swallow that.* Imagine the first sword swallower was a girl, not a man or boy like you've been told. Just a girl from your neighborhood. Imagine she's been swallowing secrets for years, sees the sword and thinks *that would be easier. More filling.* But before she can swallow the sword, she has to make room. Release her secrets. She opens her mouth, reaches in to pull out the first secret and finds it has become a broadsword. She calls it Father and puts it aside. Next, she coughs up a fencing sword she dubs Depression. She draws more swords out. Names them after the secrets they carry—half a dozen, a dozen, two dozen—until she loses count and the clang of metal on metal no longer jangles her nerves. Imagine the last one's the smallest and hardest for her to reach, lodged in her heart as it is. A sword the size of a swizzle stick. The sharpest yet. Tugging it loose, she whispers, *Mother.*

The Patient Talks of Electroshock and Lobster

Lobster is all I remember about Pop-Pop's electroshock at the hospital on South Beach. He was given lobster on the ward and liked it. I didn't visit him there, didn't see him gorge on that sweet meat after his calculated convulsions.

But lobster is what I hear a decade later when the doctor suggests electroconvulsive therapy as a way to pierce depression's seal on my skin. This is no child's play, no white glue poured over fingers, set dry, and peeled off slow. No delight in a fingerprint's lingering kiss. No thrill in traversing the stifling layers, my tongue thick with language I can no longer speak. What the doctor suggests will not do. All I can think about was Pop-Pop and the lobster. Until the lobster becomes the ECT machine becomes the lobster, and I picture my skin angry like a lobster's tail post-boil.

Now, lobsters can be shocked to death. The CrustaStun can knock a lobster out in .3 seconds, kill it in less than 10. More humane than boiling, the device shortens the lobster's suffering by minutes.

If my depression could have been cured that quickly, I would have said yes. Yes to the current to lighten my mood. Yes to the lobster.

The Sea Cucumber

after Elizabeth Bishop

Each year is the same—rows of boys
and rows of girls line both sides
of the hall. Hushed walk to the waiting
bus. Dark green seats still stick to skin.

It's November. Insects scream loud
as car horns. No respite from Miami's
heat. Teachers count students *one-two-three,*
sit, then talk to parents—chaperones

who would rather be anywhere else.
The aquarium isn't far, but the drive
seems long. Kim and Jen make friendship
bracelets and a fight almost breaks out

between two of the boys—Jimmy's kicking
the back of Travis' seat. Each time the driver
hits a pothole, everyone's heads
come close to hitting the roof of the bus.

We're thirteen bottles of beer from the end
of the song when we lurch to a stop
in front of the Seaquarium. The noise level
rises as excited yells are carried forward

in a tidal wave of sound before we get off
the bus and back in lines. Let loose
upon the grounds, we ignore commands
of *walk, don't run,* and fling ourselves into the park.

Our group meanders past the dolphin enclosure,
the stingray exhibit, and the alligators
to Discovery Bay, where we learn about sea turtles,
tropical birds, and the other creatures

that inhabit Florida's mangrove forests.
The guide shows off starfish and sea urchins,
calls them echinoderms, which means "spiny skin."
Then she picks up what looks like wet dog poop.

Cries of *gross* ring through our group, but we step
closer as she explains this sea cucumber can eject
its internal organs for protection and then grow
them back. They expel their own guts, turn inside

out, in order to tangle or confuse their prey with sticky
filaments. Nothing else measures up the rest of the trip.
On the ride home, we all yell out our favorite animal.
No one mentions the sea cucumber for fear

of not seeming cool. It's as though those of us
who liked them best now share a secret language
all our own. One of shy excitement. A lexicon
based on knowing how to let go. How to survive.

How to Be a Survivor

Understand it's not about coming out
unscathed. Look to the gingko.
A living fossil, it's been through more
than we can dream of with our rootless
feet. Our leafless limbs. Six gingko trees
survived the bombs sent to fell Hiroshima,
sheltered under the parasol of the mushroom
cloud that bloomed above the city. They dug
in. Said no. Insisted on witnessing,
on bearing testimony. Accepted their scars
as proof they'd been through *something*.
Flung open leaves like fans to keep cool
in summer. Dyed their hair bright yellow
each fall to infuse themselves with the warmth
of a dying sun. Didn't linger over each precious
leaf fall. Didn't portion their pain out piece
by piece. Learned to let go all at once.

Before the Quiet, the Storm

Beyond my basement
window, a furious flurry

falls. The trees wear
their skeletons on the outside.

White line of snow bone
clings to trunk and limb.

A quilt of quiet covers
the restive street.

What if death
is not the absence

of sound,
but its opposite?

After dinner I push
a white tablet

the size of a baby
tooth past firm grip

of foil and cardstock
into my waiting hand.

It's my 24th attempt
to lasso the thoughts

that urge early endings.
Explain to my therapist

that maybe it's silence
I crave, not an exit.

As a kid I sought
stillness by laying

flat as a flounder
at the bottom

of the pool, a friend
standing square

on my back, her feet
holding me in place

until my held
breath gave out,

until I was forced
to breach the surface.

The Patient Attempts to Explain Cutting

1.

tug of undertow
the roil and churn

2.

buried metronome
thumping the drum

3.

tiptoe of ants on tile
dash dash dash dash dash

4.

scrape of barnacles
on scales, fish flesh

5.

sawgrass strand
teeth on edge

6.

tender white tulip
petal breaking red

Heart Patience

My mother just called to tell me my father's in the ICU.
His heart's not working right. Emergency surgery.
Two stents to open the path to or from that muscle.

For the past month, I've knitted and purled strands of red,
pink, and purple wool into tiny hearts to stitch together,
stuff, and give away. I've become a surgeon of yarn.

Here's what I know of hearts: they are two fishhooks kissing,
barbs pointing downward, a promise of pain.

The Truth Is

When I was a little girl, maybe four or five, I watched movies on my bedroom wall. Far across the sea of yellow shag carpet I'd sit cross-legged and hunched over on my bed. The truth is they were not real. The truth is I saw them, still. Even though there was no machine showing a world that didn't exist, no film wrapped around a reel like a belt around a fist.

The Eyes of God Were Watching

I was afraid to close my eyes,
scared He'd get me in bed—
my thin body covered
by a sheet with Peanuts characters.

Every night I'd scream, but no one ever came.

I wondered if I was making
any noise at all—my throat
raw with disappointment.

No one came.
Not my mother.
Not my father.

God watched me for months—
eyes two pinpricks of light—glaring
down from the ceiling's light fixture.

When I told him who was watching,
my father waited until dark,
turned out the lights,
and tracked the eyes to their source—
a reflection cast by my nightlight.

Maybe my father fixed it
out of love, or maybe he was worried
God would see what he was doing.

In Therapy, the Patient Is Asked to Define: Bundle

bundle (bun - del) n. mass of bones, muscles, nerves, flesh held in place only by clothes.

Use it in a sentence:

When I was seventeen, after having me recite the names of the first five books of Moses, my seventy-year-old Rabbi called me a "bundle of sex."

Write a poem using each letter of the word as the first letter of each line:

Bundle

Bible study
under your
nebbishy gaze—
deliver me from this
lecherous
exodus from reason.

Each Night the Girl Makes a New Resolution

Tonight I'll be a dust mote on the red desk. An ant crawling outside the house. Tonight I'll slip between my shadow and yours. Lock my door. Hide in the closet. Cover myself with caution tape. Bathe in trash. Tonight I'll be the rabbit's heartbeat and quivering nose. I'll pretend I'm dead. Pretend I'm on Mars. Tonight I'll forget.

Tonight I'll speak in tongues. Tonight I'll fly at you—become a hundred palmetto bugs. Sting you like a jellyfish. Watch from the ceiling. Film everything. Take notes. Hide inside a book. Call on God. Jesus. Buddha. Kali. Granny. Tonight I'll forget.

Tonight you'll cry before. During. After. Tonight you'll admit you've done wrong. You'll stop. You'll stop. You'll stop. Tonight I'll forget.

Tonight you'll stay the fuck away. Get help. Get me help. Tonight it ends. Tonight I'll fight back. Tonight I'll forget.

Tonight I'll kill you in your sleep. Tonight I'll cut myself. Swallow pills. Kill myself. Tonight I'll forget.

Tonight I'll stare you in the eyes the whole time and make you watch. Tonight I'll forget.

Tonight.

Forget.

Tonight.

The Alligator Girl Becomes

Nights the girl slips into the alligator skin
she relishes the weight of husk—how her arms
and legs fit, how the surface welcomes her,
wraps her frame in its reptilian hug.

She remembers countless field trips
to the Everglades, her classmates shrieking
as the gator's mouth was held shut by
the guide's hand, proof of man's superiority.

She felt bad for the creature, on display
against its will for kids who would kill
it rather than listen to the soul song
of its bellows. The gator's cold eyes

always drew her in. Her mother says
the girl's skin is too thin. A gator's hide
is thick. Impervious. She still hasn't figured out
how to work the eyelids. She'll need them

to swim with her eyes open for predators.
For prey. Nights she dreams of flight
she understands she is becoming.
She's tapped into the genetic memory

of that common ancestor that kept her kind
close to the earth but saw her kin take to the skies.
They learned a different kind of freedom.
She grows adept at flicking her tail,

clacking her jaws, the high walk
and low crawl. Practices her log
imitation in the bathtub, snout
above water, breathing in. Out.

The night she leaves for good,
she tries on the prom dress her mother
bought after making her lose
fifteen pounds in time to get a date.

She smooths the dress down, enjoys
the slide of satin over scale, each bump
still visible through fabric. Her mother
would tell her to hide the lumps with Spanx.

The girl twirls for the bathroom mirror
one last time, then shreds the dress
with her claws. She won't need it where
she's going—back to the swamps.

She lowers first her head, then her front
and back legs into the toilet bowl, her diving
form a perfect ten, and with a snap of her tail,
she flushes herself away, leaves not a trace.

Her Childhood Home

The flamingo feathers its nest with sawgrass and stones
The rabbit that visits each day at four is found dead next
To the monkey's cage the father's hand is far too fond
Of the daughter's breast her bedroom carpet the color
Of just-shed blood and the mother whacks the daughter
One hundred times each night with a brush so her hair
Shines brighter than the Big Dipper in the April sky
The stars are always there glaring down at her during
The day she sees them each time she faints and each time
She turns the lights off in her bedroom God's eyes bore
Through her and pin her to the bed where she screams
For help she dreams of leaving even her turtle ran away

The Patient Admits

I could not stand waiting for my father
to come through my bedroom door,
cross over the red carpet I begged for
after the roof leaked and ruined
the repulsive yellow shag that covered
the top floor of the house, so he could
get into bed with me. How many nights
did I spend waiting? Some I fell asleep
before he stumbled into my room. Others
I clutched my Peanuts sheet as tight
as I could for protection. I counted sheep.
Counted breath. Counted the bumps
on the popcorn ceiling until he'd stagger
down the long hallway, and I'd stay as still
as possible and hope he would go straight
into his bedroom. The one next to mine.
The one furthest from mom's. Sometimes
that worked. And sometimes it didn't.
And the waiting. The waiting. Imagine
knowing the exact moment an accident
will kill your children or being told the day
but not the month, not the year you will die,
and you are helpless to stop it. Or avoid it.
So, one time, just once, you seek it out.
Because you can't take the waiting anymore.
So one night, I walked across the red carpet
to stand in the open door of my father's bedroom.
Empty. I trudged the length of the yellow shag
hallway, passed my mother's closed bedroom door,
tiptoed down the twenty stairs to the foyer

with the ugly mustard linoleum, turned to enter
the monochrome den, saw my father asleep
and snoring on the rough commercial carpet
my mother insisted on buying even though it hurt
to sit on, the television humming snow, and (just once,
just once, I swear, just once) whispered, *Dad.*

The Patient's Aversion to Bananas Begins

The light inside the office felt trapped. Above us,
plastic panels clutching fluorescent tubes pulsed.
The office never changed: a large print with a path

to draw the eyes past the forest in the foreground.
Potted plant. Tissue box. Chair. Couch.
The therapist asked if I was ready.

> *The average height of a father is seventy inches.*

I sat in the same awkward triangle with my mother
the week before. No, I wasn't ready to do this again.

> *The average height of a toddler is thirty-six inches.*

I stared at a spot on the ceiling, an old water stain
or trick of light, I'm not sure. That day, I swear I saw
a face, a Rorschach portrait waiting to be unlocked.

> *The average length of a small banana is six inches.*

This was my time of rebellion. My time of *no*.
Nineteen, dropped out of college, my parents desperate
to know why, and me too scared to confront them.

> *Things a toddler might want to lick:* her mother's breasts,
> a popsicle, an electrical outlet, dirt, a board book,
> a set of keys, an ash tray, the dog's nose.

I fixed on the forest in the print, imagined the reaction
of my father and therapist if I stood up, crossed over
the room, climbed into the scene, and left them behind.

> *Things a teenager might expect a father to say*
> *in response to allegations of abuse:* "How dare you!"
> "I love my daughter. I could never hurt her."

What my father said: "When she was two or three,
she saw me naked on the bed. She asked what my penis was.
I said it was a banana. Then I asked her if she wanted to lick it."

Attempts at Flight

Already, I am mid-flight.
So I tell myself to stay, that *this* is not *that*, remind myself
of where I am. Touch something real. The back of the couch,
perhaps. Feel how the fabric is soft and textured and *here*.
Return to the moment, a bird back to the wire,
feathers askew. Resettle.

And for a while it's good. I touch the couch
when I feel flighty. It reminds me of what's real. I don't look
out the window. The robins won't help. They know what to do.
How to do it. And by looking, I am leaving. So, in the moment,
I stay.

Until I push her hand away
and apologize I'm sorry I'm sorry I'm sorry
because how do I explain or
allow her to continue, steel myself.

And the words *steel myself* have no place
in lovemaking or sex or even fucking. Because the birds outside
are flying and I want to fly, oh how I want to fly, and so I touch
the couch, I touch her, I try to hold on because if I let go I will fall.
I touch the couch, memorize the bumps of the fabric, remind
myself why I am here. That this is supposed to be good.
I am good.

This moment with the woman and the couch and the birds
is good. And I know that birds don't steel themselves to fly,
they just lift, and I want to lift.

But I am tethered
to this body that remembers, so I steel myself
because I somehow still have hope, and I take control
for a while because sometimes it's easier to help someone fly
than to fly myself, so I make sure that she flies and flies and flies.

Self-Portrait of the Patient as a Murmuration of Starlings

I fingerprint the sky

Take the nearest exit
My Borg brain

& its multitudes
& its voices

(& *they are legion*)
)& *they are without relent*(

Become portent

What I'm trying to say is
What I'm trying to say is

I seek a guidance system

To be pilot not passenger
Primal not prey

Nails

This is a poem
about how my mother

got her nails done   switched off. How
each week   her replacement
by a Cuban woman   self switched on,
named Marta—   dragged me up
                                                             the stairs,
                                                             screaming.
                                                             The way she'd dig

the crescent moons
of her French manicure

shiny like bone   into my scalp.
stripped
of muscle and sinew.

How victory

for her   for me was tallied
was getting through   if my fingers found
the next   the broken strips
                                                             of her nails

hours

without ruining   later. The scabs
the work she'd paid   their grip left
to have done.   behind.

                                                             The antlers that
                                                             grew in their place
                                                             like bright tines
                                                             poking
                                                             through leaves
                                                             on a forest floor.

Two Objects[1] and a Girl

I.

At breakfast the girl spits out gazelle fur with every sip of tea. It clings to the walls, her saliva like glue. Gets stuck between her teeth. At night she coughs up more hair balls than the cat.

She's all instinct and scent. Smells too much of her father. He's been sniffing around. Her fur has come in and her ears grow long. She's skittish. On guard.

The girl's mother hires a dressmaker to cover her daughter's changed form, but the woman doesn't have patterns that fit the four-legged creature standing before her. She advises the mother to fashion a bed out of straw. Make the girl comfortable. *What else can you do?*

The girl knows. But her long tongue can't wrap itself around the word *flee*. The other girls call her wild and the teacher leashes her to the treadmill in gym. Over and over she runs the same course, clenches her teeth against tongue and tastes blood.

II.

One day, just like that, the girl sheds her fur. Her ears recede until they can no longer be seen, and she starts humming a lot. Her head narrows at the top and widens at the base and when struck, sounds a hollow thunk. Inside—a constant drone. She walks as though travelling through liquid gone thick and viscous.

---

1. Méret Oppenheim's "Object" (a gazelle fur covered tea cup, saucer and spoon) and "La bicyclette à la selle d'abeilles" (a photograph of a bicycle seat covered with bees)

At night, when the girl's father comes to her bed, he complains of stings.

She pedals her bike around town. Flowers bend toward her as she passes and she aches to bathe in their yellow dust. The girl is last sighted near the bus station.

The people who saw her that day swear she shimmered like a hot-road mirage. She was there and then she wasn't and the seat of her bicycle was swathed in bees.

The Body Keeps the Score

Easiest to think of it in terms
of science—of teeth and bone,

blood and tissue, muscle and fat.
Those trace elements.

Easier not to think of it at all—
to float above the plucked

cello string of my body.
Pretend I can fly off any time.

Harder to see the truth of it—
tea-kettle whistle nerves,

repeated thoughts in common time,
as practiced as scales or arpeggios.

Hardest to see the truth—
this body as more than just broken.

Its composition made intricate
and exquisite by experience.

The Blue Notebook

April 12–15, 1983

Research

Seventh grade and once a week the bus took us
gifted students from junior high to junior college.

Seventh grade and I: ran away from home, lost
two flutes and a jacket, was nicknamed Spacy.

At the library at Miami Dade Community College
I picked up a thick book about prescription drugs.

Seventh grade and amber-bottled pills stolen
from my mother's medicine cabinet. Twenty-odd

RORER 714 tablets, white and scored down
the middle—Quaaludes, the guide assured me.

The red ones I couldn't find in pages after pages
of color photos of pills—I called those *Insurance*.

The Attempt

Red pill.
White pill.
Orange juice.
White pill.
Handful of white.
Handful of red.
Chalk taste.
Choke.
Orange juice.
The urge to puke.
You have to be quiet for this to work.
Pills gone.
Lights out.

The Blue Notebook

I can't explain why I hid the folder in my closet like stolen goods, like the makeup I took from drug stores or the colored paper clips I ripped off from the campus bookstore and wore as earrings. Can't explain why I pressed the reasons for killing myself between pages of loose-leaf like flowers, like mementos of a trip, like ticket stubs from a movie. In the emergency room that morning, a curtain separating us from the doctors and nurses, I tell my father the notebook's shoved under a shoe box on the shelf above the bin he built for my toys. When I get home it's gone.

The Plum

Here's what I remember:
        just home from the hospital
the deep sigh of my body
        burrowing into the sofa.

Holding the plum
        my mother handed me
still wet from the sink.

Watching mom and dad fight.
        Their mouths moving.
That first bite. The taste.
        So unexpected. So alive.

After Stopping to Pick Up J's Birthday Present, My Father and I Take a Walk at Greynolds Park

We were blanketed in sweat. Walked past the mangroves and live oaks covered with Spanish moss, the canopy full of air plants cupping their ears to listen to our words or the call of bird song. I can't remember what you said. Maybe you asked me why I tried and maybe I told you some story explaining it away. Maybe I stayed silent as the gumbo-limbo, with its peeling, sunburnt skin, a strangler fig closing tighter and tighter around its trunk.

At J's 13th Birthday Party

I smuggle in a secret bigger than a birthday gift
covered in blue cardstock and tied with rope

thick as a wrist. Watch as the presents
are unwrapped. Listen as all the girls,

giddy and high on cake and ice cream, tease
each other about who has a crush on who.

Lift my mouth into a smile that says,
Yes, I'm having fun. See. Like a normal girl.

Just like you.

The Glass Girl Recalls Her Transformation

Something was wrong. The mirror
confirmed her suspicion—her skin was clear
as a cave pond. Her fibula and tibia suspended
from the ceiling of her calf like stalactites.

The next day her right cheek turned crystal.
Her jawbone a bell, her tongue a dumb clapper.

Next, her arms changed. Then her torso.

The girl watched the transformation
in the mirror, fascinated by the tight grasp
the fingers of her ribs kept on the fist
of her heart. The way blood pumped
through the aquarium of her body.
Her lungs, two glass sponges,
her uterus a jellyfish floating above
the seaweed of her intestines.

She bought pillows with her allowance,
duct taped them under her clothes to stop
herself from shattering. Ignored the calls
of *Fatso!* as she waddled the halls of school.

She wanted to yell back, ask for help,
but when she opened her mouth—
only the clink of champagne flutes came out.

When the girl's conversion was complete,
she stared at herself in the full-length mirror
stripped of padding and clothes, and realized,
in certain light, she could not be seen. At all.

That was the day she left home for good,
the day she walked right past her parents
still arguing about what to do with her,
and onto the street where she followed
the telephone lines stretching on for miles.

The Patient

culled from my psychiatric admission notes dated February 2000

was evaluated.
is living.
relates to depression.
reports that she takes her dog for a walk.
rarely eats lunch.
reports no initial difficulty.
has experienced decreased, passive, worsening.
describes mood.
has had active thoughts but not acted.
describes ten prior episodes.
did overdose.
was taken.
does recall a history of childhood.
has experienced behaviors and symptoms.
began treatment.
has not found this helpful.
was prescribed Zoloft.
was prescribed Prozac.
was prescribed Wellbutrin.
was prescribed Effexor.
was restarted.
has used.
reports a positive family history.
was adopted.
was raised.
does recall significant conflict.
recalls school.
reports abuse.

did not enjoy.
left home.
recalls feeling.
has been residing.
denies any significant history.
is notable.
demonstrates decreased, blunted, anxious.
demonstrates thought processes.
denies current, active abnormalities.
is constricted.
is alert and oriented.
will meet to discuss benefits.
may do well with aggressive treatment.
should agree.

The Patient's Complaint

Anything I say will be held against me. This complaint for instance.
You'll label me non-compliant for complaining. I may be held. There
are restraints for that. Medicine. Jackets. Rooms. But I swear, I'm only
moving two letters around. I-A-N-T. A-I-N-T. The beginning's still the
same. C-O-M-P-L. As in complementary: things that go well together.
Complimentary: words we use when we think someone has done well
or if we like their choice of clothing. I'm a fan of jackets, but I'm afraid
I can't compliment yours. Bright white doesn't complement my skin
tone. One of the boxes the nurse ticked off about me when I checked
into the hospital was unkempt. And it's true. I could not keep up.

Non compos mentis. Not of sound mind. Non-compl-iant. Non-
compl-aint. Ain't. I'm sounding ignorant. But I'm not. I just can't
think fast right now. My brain has thickened to gravy. I can't swim
through the thoughts to get to the other side. The other side has left
the building. I can't leave the building. There are locks and checks and
double checks. And there's fresh air outside, anyway, on the 12 foot by
12 foot enclosed patio with the two picnic benches and the thirty-odd
patients filtering in and out to smoke and remind themselves that there
is a world beyond the 15-minute checks at night and the compulsory
classes on managing anger or sadness or your shoes without their
laces. Wouldn't want us to try anything. Wouldn't want us to be non-
compliant.

And if you do. If you, say, try to hang yourself with your bed sheets
knotted and tied to the bathroom door, push both beds against the
door to the room while I am off on the patio smoking, expect me to feel
guilty I wasn't there to stop you. Expect me to scream for a nurse when
I get to the door I can't open all the way and see your face purpling
above the white sheets tied tight around your neck. Expect boxes to be

ticked off. Expect to be moved to a ward with one-on-one observation. Expect to be labeled non-compliant. But don't expect me to complain or follow your lead.

My complaints have not made it past my gravy-thick brain to my mouth, my voice. I'm voiceless. My speech: sluggish. My affect: flat. Blunted. There is no there, there. I've disappeared. I couldn't complain even if I wanted to, but I don't. Want to, that is. Because I've done this before. I know the quickest way out is to be compliant. Take what's offered. Pills. Therapy. Even though they don't work. Haven't ever worked. The cure is an illusion. The hospital is an allusion. Each state a different hospital. Each hospital the same state. The same staff. The same game. You want to leave? Be compliant. Don't complain.

No Peace

In December 1986, Carlos Paz Jr., an 18-year-old high school student,
shot his mother, father, and 10-year-old sister to death in their Miami
Lakes, FL, home. We were friends.

Your last name means peace.

*

December and the streets are slick with rain that won't stop.
December and you try to buy a handgun.
When you are turned away, you buy a rifle. Any gun will do.
December and the floors of your home are thick with blood.

*

The jacarandas, cabbage palms, and gumbo limbos
            heave outside in the dense air. No break
from growing. The teeming tourists are angry—
their beach dreams rain delayed. On TV, the newscaster
says the words *family, murdered,*
                        Miami Lakes, looking, Carlos Paz, call,
                                                suspect.
I defend you to the cool room. I'm alone,
and I hear no reply.
Even the trees outside are quiet.

*

It's 1986, and I'm well-acquainted with anger,
but my dreams of death were forged in fire:
my mother in her bed or my father in his van.

*

Carlos, I think the last time I saw you
was at our piano teacher's house.
                              Your sister,
Alina, a limp doll asleep in your lap,
          the scene evoked: a reversed pietà.

*

You are now the age your mom and dad
                  were when you killed them.
At night, in prison, do you dream
          of being shot by children you'll never have?

*

Or maybe the last time we spoke
was at the party you threw
—your parents and sister out of town
or out for the night, all of us drinking,
scent of a joint wafting in from outside.

We sat on the couch, smoked cigarettes,
while a record played Phil Collins'
"In the Air Tonight." You told me
he wrote it after his friend drowned
while someone stood by and watched.

*

I remember hearing that you killed your sister
        so she wouldn't have to live with what you'd done.

*

My father's van caught fire
soon after I dreamt it would.
He wasn't hurt, but it scared
me enough that I went back
to only dreaming of escape.

*

Were you certain you could kill when you bought the rifle
or as you pulled the trigger that first time?

And who was first? Your father, the real target of your rage,
or your mother who stood by, or the sister

                                 you wanted to protect?
And how did it feel, knowing you murdered the man

whose name you carry? The woman who gave birth to you?
The sister who looked up to you?

*

It is just another rainy Friday in December, and the Paz family is
hosting a tree-trimming party. Carlos and Alina play a Christmas duet
on the piano in the living room and everyone applauds. The guests all
comment on how handsome Carlos has become, ask him about school
and his girlfriend. His future plans. They pat Alina on her head, talk
about what a great beauty she'll be and how smart she is, just like her

mother. They ask the family if they will travel during the holiday or stay home. The guests gather their raincoats and umbrellas, head out to their cars. The family of four stands just outside the front door, arms linked round each other, waving goodbye.

*

That was the night you killed them.

*

I know from experience
          the walls of townhouses are thick.
No one ever heard my screams,
          or if they did, they ignored them.
I wonder if your neighbors heard
          or ignored what happened
all those years you said you were abused.

*

Carlos,
                    You were eighteen.

                              Why didn't you just leave?

The Patient Attempts to Explain PTSD with Time Travel Theory

Draw two dots, six inches apart, on a sheet of paper.

Label the first dot childhood (or substitute a time in your life that haunts you).

Label the second dot with your name and location. Include the current day, date and time.

Draw a line between the two dots. Call this linear time. It travels from point A (the past) to point B (which is always right now).

Call this good. Call it the past staying where it belongs.

Fold the paper in half so the two dots line up exactly.

Take a pencil or other pointed object and punch a hole from point A through to point B. See how the distance between the dots shrank from six inches to barely a whisper in an instant?

Call this what you have been trying to avoid. Call this the triggering event.

Leave the newly created portal open. Picture a tunnel connecting the once vast distance between points in this folded space. Call it a wormhole. Call it an Einstein-Rosen Bridge.

Call it being unable to tell the difference between past and present.

Call it being in your living room in 2013 and feeling the brush your
    mother beat you with in 1975 strike your head over and over.
    Call it smelling your father's aftershave everywhere. Call it
    feeling his fingers stroke your cheek just as he did each night he
    got into bed with you when you were ten.

Call it what it is. A flashback. Time travel.

The Patient Experiences a Flashback for the First Time

We were on your parent's couch and your skin smelled like marijuana
and lake water warmed by the Miami sun and your mouth tasted
like vanilla fudge swirl, tasted better than any ice cream
I'd ever tried and you liked me—you said so after we graduated—
and I realized you hadn't asked me to prom to be ironic, and I was sorry
I'd said no, and it was the last summer before we left for college
and I wanted to be there with you and you wanted to be there with me
and that was enough, and we kissed and it was good you were on top,
your weight comforting like a heavy blanket on a cold night
and we were kissing and the air conditioning couldn't cool the heat
colliding off our bodies and then you were not you
anymore—you were him—and I couldn't figure out why my father
was on me, was on your parent's sofa in the middle of the day smelling
of pot and lake and then you swam back to me for a second and we kept
kissing but already it was ruined, and his face kept floating in front
of my eyes and his hands were your hands were his hands and your
mouth was his mouth and his tongue was your tongue was his tongue
and then you were asking me, or he was asking me, if it was okay
and it wasn't but I couldn't talk without water rushing in
and I was submerged and frantic, clawing toward sky, when I finally
sputtered something that made you freeze, and my breathing was ragged
from being dragged free of the undertow, and I just said I couldn't
but I never told you why I made you stop, why I was drowning.

Walking South Beach after Hurricane David, 1979

Sunbaked place of burial and resurrection. Seaweed strewn shoreline glinting with inflated iridescent bladders and trailing tentacles of washed-up Portuguese men-o-war. Scrubbed clean of tourists on this sun blotted September day. Beach snarled with flotsam, sea tangle, razor sharp shells of crabs. Salt water stung palm trees snapped in half. Driftwood daggered in the blonde grit. The stench of rot looming. And seagulls feasting on fish flung from the ocean's gut, their twisted bodies and unblinking eyes stunned at the sudden fury of home.

In Therapy, the Patient Is Asked to Define: Polaroid

Polaroid (poh-la-roid) n. quickly developing image forever seared in memory.

Use it in a sentence:

Dressed as Charlie Chaplin for a junior high party, I reached into the pocket of the coat I borrowed from my father and pulled out three Polaroids of a naked woman lying on my mother's bed.

Write a poem using each letter of the word as the first letter of each line:

Polaroid

Posed naked
on my mother's bed
lies a woman—she's
as open as my mouth is
right now.
Oh, daddy—tell me how
I am supposed to
dance tonight.

The Patient Attempts to Describe Her Experience with Depakote

Imagine your head filled with. No.
That's not right. First, imagine a house.
A townhouse. Upstairs: three bedrooms
and two baths. Downstairs: a living room.
Galley kitchen. Dining room. Den. Foyer.
Half bath. Fill these rooms with a small
family. A mother. A father. A daughter.

See the girl dress for school. The mother
dress for tennis. The father dress for sales
calls. The mother writes checks for bills.
Makes stained glass. The father builds
a dollhouse for the girl. Types and mails
resume after resume. See the girl practice
piano. Color. Watch TV after homework.

Father watches the girl watch TV. Mother
watches father watch the girl. Mother drags
the girl upstairs by her hair. The girl plucks
mother's just-manicured nails from her scalp
one-by-one. Father fucks another woman
in mother's bed. The girl sits in her closet.
Reads a book. Drinks vodka. Again. Again.

Father and mother fight. Mother and girl
fight. Girl fights father off. Father fights
to stay in the girl's bed. Mother and father
and girl fight. Mother rages. Mother leaves.

Comes back. Girl is there is not there
does not cannot leave. Father leaves. Girl
realizes leaving isn't possible. Is not leaving.

Picture everything that happened there
in that house portrayed on endless loop
at full volume on the projection screen
of your mind. The daughter. Her father.
Her mother. A constant stream. A TV playing
every channel at same time at full volume.
Or ten TVs. A hundred. Now, pull the plug.

The Patient Decides She Wants to Live

But no one explains what to expect. How to court life. She's spent too many years chasing death. Knows too much about endings. How trees make appealing targets. Their solid stillness. Death as a comfort food. As security blanket. The ultimate protection. Without that cloak she's exposed. Raw. Her nerves scorch and flare like the sunburn she got that time at the beach reading a fantasy book for hours without moving in a sand chair. The nausea and dizziness that followed. The pain. How five weeks later a classmate asked if she was wearing red tights. She thinks living will be like hugging barbed wire. First the steel bite and surge of blood. Then the scab.

In Therapy, the Patient Is Asked to Define: Alimony

alimony (al - i - moh - nee) n. a bribe given by a parent to the child they pretended was their spouse for continued silence and complicity.

Use it in a sentence:

I received the alimony check from my father today; the extra hundred bucks will pay for another session of therapy.

Write a poem using each letter of the word as the first letter of each line:

Alimony

All those nights I
lie there,
I was forced to snap
myself
out of my body.
Now,
you will pay.

Hialeah Apocalypse

Each morning I woke to sea urchins shedding
their spines, leaving a trail of needles in their wake
and starfish congregating in constellations
echoed by the night sky. Bioluminescent jellyfish
swarmed the shore. Stingrays turned fanned backs
to the coast like a quiver of arrows hurtling
into the Bermuda Triangle.

That November the sky was scrubbed free of stars
for seven days and every skyscraper, every palm tree
clawed at empty space, desperate for guidance. Every
shrimp-smudged flamingo disappeared. The squeaky
windshield wipers of my father's Dodge Omni, my mother's
stained glass supplies and every line on every tennis court
at Milander Park. All of them, gone, gone, gone.
The air thick with smoke and glass.

I dreamed the palm trees, their fingers
feathered like a child's eyelashes, invited me outside
where the humid night glittered with suspended shards.
I reached out for one and another and another and tried
to puzzle-piece them back in place, but there were too many
fragments and none of them fit right in their frames.

That year I broke my leg on a see-saw, but I never spoke
to God and because of that now I talk to everything.
Strangers. Piano keys. The oyster's knife edge.

Listen

Listen. The cicadas just turned on. They're stuttering something about summer, trying to remember its taste after the long cycle of dreaming electric drone, as if trapped under wires carrying current. Sound of all is well, sound of home. Until some background hum calls them, blinking, from the earth every seventeen years.

Listen as the starling caught in the chimney's throat beats its small music against brick. Hollow bones, unanswered echoes. Listen to how the mouth of the fireplace releases a scuffle of Morse code a *tap tap ruffle scratch* until exhausted, the bird settles, warbles good night.

On Silent Retreat at the Abbey of Gethsemani

—Trappist, Kentucky

I learn that silence suits me. That I want to be as quiet
as two sulphur butterflies dancing above mid-May's
sweet peas. I crave the kind of peace that allows me
to hear my thoughts or realize those brief moments
when I haven't been having any thoughts. Silence
of forgetting. Of remembering. The hush when I look
through the lens and all that matters is my camera,
my held breath, and whatever I'm trying to capture.
I learn that maybe noise isn't the problem. I like
the liquid *glug-glug-glee* of the brown-headed cowbird
and the insistent murmur of bees. The call of the bells,
of thunder rumbling in the distance, and the hum
of a helicopter. The mumble of monks chanting.
I recognize calm in a blade of grass, the far off knobs
cresting above the land, an empty bench on a hillside.
The sun's sulkiness on a grey spring day, the steadfastness
of a stone wall. The stillness of a new cross in the Abbey
cemetery. Of a statue or a far-off silo. A blinking traffic
signal and no cars for miles, an unthreatened chipmunk,
or an empty hummingbird feeder. Or the hold a seedpod
has on a Kentucky coffeetree all winter and into spring.
Of the moment that seedpod relinquishes its grip.

Serotiny

in the deep forest of my body:

a pinecone: seeds packed tight:

patient as the universe

before that big bang: imagine:

all those comets and planets,

all the stars and dark matter,

in the smallest waiting room:

my heart: my pinecone:

be ready: when that freeing fire

blazes toward you: at the first

sign of scorched earth—burst forth

The Girl Stripped Bare

*Marcel Duchamp's "The Bride Stripped
Bare by Her Bachelors, Even" or "The Large Glass"*
—Philadelphia Museum of Art

Here we see the bride. Here we see through the bride. She is glass. Framed. Shattered. Here is a girl. She is eleven or twelve. She is made of glass. You can see right through her. She sees the bride. She sees the bachelors. When she steps past the frame, she is shattered. The bride is not made of glass. She is not glass. She is not not-glass. She is metal. Shattered. (Im)patient. She was framed. She is waiting. The bride conducts her bachelors. The bride stripped bare. The bride was stripped bare. The bride strips the bachelors. The bachelors are bare. The bride is shattered.

Here are the bride's bachelors, waiting. They are in line. They are made of lines. They line up. They are (im)patient. They are metal and glass and shattered. They cannot spin through the air. Their wings are pinned. They are flattened between pages of glass. The bride is out of reach. She is stripped bare. They stripped her, bare. The girl is also here. She watches the bachelors. She is (im)patient. She does not like lines. She does not like the bachelors. She is made of glass. She longs to be stripped bare, shattered. She has been framed. She has been stripped bare. Shattered.

Memory

Backseat driver who urges you to speed up
at the bend in the road you've never taken
and ignores caution. She's been there before.

Sports Doc Martens, spiked green hair, tattoos,
a frilly dress and won't take any more of your shit.

Balances a spoon on the edge of her nose to get
your attention. Never learned to swim, only knows
how to be a fish. Disappears fast around corners.

Reads your future in your cells, knows which freckle
will make the doctor call you into her office,
ask you to sit. Refuses to go to the appointment.

Races, smart rat that she is, through the maze
of your brain with certainty that comes from years
of practice. She gnaws through walls that don't
give way, intent always on the treat at the end.

Saunters into a bar, orders bourbon neat and sits
on a sticky stool waiting for you to ask her out.

Travels while you sleep, breakfasts in the caves
at Lascaux, sunbathes near the pyramids, takes
tea in Morocco. Sends frenzied dreams of want.

Abandons you on the way home from school,
in the grocery store, on the playground. Laughs
because you are still there, stranded and scared.

Dives deeper than the SCUBA instructor said
was possible on one tank of oxygen, ignores
your careful tables, your math of safety, never
worries about the bends, never caves to pressure.

Corkscrews her way through your life, leaves behind
stray bits of bark, renders the wine undrinkable.

Smokes pot on Haight St., beats a bongo out of rhythm,
begs on a street corner holding a hand-lettered sign:
WILL WORK SOMETIMES, RARELY WHEN NEEDED.

Pulls your pigtails then taps you on your left shoulder
but when you look over your right (sure you know
her tricks) you discover she was never there at all.

Peers out from the cover of woods, patient wolf lying
in wait. Fails to mention the rabbit she is hunting is you.

Mala Madre, or Song of the Abused Daughter

My roommate calls the spider plant
    I bought *mala madre*—bad mother.
Says she'll throw her babies out
    but keep the umbilical cord tied
tight. Says we're a perfect match.

        Bad mother, spider mother.
        Toss your babies overboard.

I bring my bad mother everywhere,
    hang her in the corner—perfect
balance of sun and shade. Water
    her often. She comments on
everything I do—her whisper sharp.

        Bad mother, spider mother.
        You did what you could.

Her leaves stretch toward me
    like fingers when I pass nearby.
She likes to yank my hair—
    reminds me how she would drag
me up the stairs by my ponytail.

        Bad mother, spider mother.
        I have to let you go.

We live like this for years—my bad
    mother, my spider mother, and me.
Until I move again and leave her
    suspended by the wall's embrace,
thirsty and calling my name.

Moving to San Francisco, I Visit Laura and Alex and We Take a Canoe Out on a Frozen Lake to Check on Her Science Experiment

—Concord, New Hampshire, November 1992

We power through wrist-thick ice until we hit water
then pull and hope the canoe's prow gains purchase.

Dig and drag even as our wooden paddles splinter
and shred and fingers of fog hide our heavy breath.

Our grunts and the paddles punching the only sounds
on this empty lake until we send chunks of ice singing

across its crystalline surface. Landfall comes sudden
as winter. On the damp, peaty ground, wintergreen's

red berries and dark, waxy leaves poke through fall's
detritus. I gather and crush a bunch in my ungloved hand,

inhale the scent of starting over. Paper birches scratch
reminders of their old selves on the clear November sky.

And before we leave, I look back at the lake we crossed
to see our path sealing shut like a coat zipping closed.

Suitcases

All the children whose mothers threatened to take them back to the orphanage were left standing at the bottom of the stairs, fast-packed suitcases in hand, facing the door with hope for the first time in their short lives. Someone (not their mothers) opened the door for them and they all (every single one) stepped through and into the bright sun. Some of the children went mad and were never heard from again.

The remaining children walked east toward the ocean, guarded by armies of armadillos during the day and concealed at night under blankets of bats. They slept tucked in a hug of mangrove root after eating ice cream mangoes, and were watched over by Key deer. In the morning, the swamp rabbits gave up some of their lettuce to the children for breakfast.

The children knew to keep the siren call of the manatee, which sounded a lot like a pinky swear made with your very best friend, on their left and the line of palm trees ushering them forward on their right. Some of the children cried as they walked, each tear attracting a tiny tadpole as it hit the asphalt, while others complained about the blisters on their feet and the weight of their suitcases until (when they weren't looking) someone came by and strung a balloon to their fingers and the handles of their suitcases, allowing them to float along the path, and some sang songs that spilled out of their mouths like bubbles but filled with candies to eat and small toys to play with on their walk.

These children who had never been in an orphanage stopped by one along the way to see what it was like. They didn't (in fact) like what they saw, so they freed the orphan children who followed along after them, singing and complaining and crying in turn.

When the children whose mothers threatened to take them back to the orphanage arrived at the ocean, the adults on the beach stared and whispered and threatened to call the Division of Children's Services, but the children knew what they had to do and got to work, first fashioning a giant castle in the sand, with spires and turrets and dungeons galore (where they put any adult who looked like they might cause trouble) and a drawbridge that reached far across the ocean to a distant land.

Then, two-by-two, hand-in-hand, these children whose mothers threatened to take them back to the orphanage they had never come from in the first place (and the actual orphans they'd liberated along the way) walked across the sea, never once looking back.

On Going Home

I am the fish
caught and released

and caught again.
I always take the bait.

A hundred holes
freckle my fragile mouth.

Each time, I return
convinced I won't be

seduced by the wiggling
worm's easy flesh,

won't be surprised
by the barbed tang of hook.

Acknowledgments

With gratitude to the editors of the journals who first published these poems, sometimes in slightly different versions.

Bellevue Literary Review: "The Patient"

Cider Press Review: "The Patient's Aversion to Bananas Begins"

The Collagist: "The Patient Decides She Wants to Live"

Crab Orchard Review: "Hialeah Apocalypse"

Deaf Poets Society: "In Therapy, the Patient Is Asked to Define: Alimony" and "The Patient Attempts to Describe Her Experience with Depakote"

diode poetry journal: "The Patient's Complaint" and "The Patient Talks of Electroshock and Lobster"

Gingerbread House Literary Journal: "Suitcases"

Glass: A Journal of Poetry: "How to Be a Survivor"

Greensboro Review: "The Truth Is"

Hairstreak Butterfly Review: "No Peace" and "Walking South Beach after Hurricane David, 1979"

Lambda Literary Review Spotlight: "Heart Patience"

The Louisville Review: "*Mala Madre,* or Song of the Abused Daughter"

Mid-American Review: "The Glass Girl Recalls Her Transformation"

Moon City Review: "The Alligator Girl Becomes"

Muzzle Magazine: "Two Objects and a Girl" and "Her Childhood Home"

New Plains Review: "On Silent Retreat at the Abbey of Gethsemani"

North Dakota Quarterly: "The Patient Attempts to Explain Cutting"

Pittsburgh Poetry Review: "Nails"

Rogue Agent: "The Body Keeps the Score"

Room Magazine: "The Secret Swallower Reveals Her Swords"

Rust + Moth: "The Patient Admits"

Sinister Wisdom: "The Blue Notebook" and "The Sea Cucumber"

South Dakota Review: "The Girl Stripped Bare"

Southern Humanities Review: "Serotiny"

Still: The Journal: "Moving to San Francisco, I Visit Laura and Alex and We Take a Canoe Out on a Frozen Lake to Check on Her Science Experiment"

Stirring: "Listen"

Thrush Poetry Journal: "Before the Quiet, the Storm"

Tinderbox Poetry Journal: "Each Night the Girl Makes a New Resolution," "The Eyes of God Were Watching," "In Therapy, the Patient Is Asked to Define: Polaroid," and "Self Portrait of the Patient as a Murmuration of Starlings"

Washington Square Review: "The Patient Attempts to Explain PTSD with Time Travel Theory"

Whale Road Review: "On Going Home"

WomenArts Quarterly Journal: "Memory"

Yemassee: "Attempts at Flight"

With Gratitude

So many people have lent their eyes and ears to the poems that comprise this manuscript over the last six years. I want to acknowledge those who have helped me get to the point where this manuscript is ready to be published with editorial help, mentorship, funding, and friendship.

Thank you to the following organizations for their support and belief in me and my work: National Endowment for the Arts, Kentucky Foundation for Women, Barbara Deming Memorial Fund, Edward Albee Foundation, New York Mills Regional Cultural Center, Ragdale Foundation, Sundress Academy for the Arts (SAFTA) and Firefly Farm, Vermont Studio Center, Appalachian Writers Workshop, Kentucky Women Writers Conference, and the Mountain Heritage Literary Festival.

Thank you to the following people for their help and encouragement with the poems that are included in this manuscript:

At Southern Illinois University: Judy Jordan, Allison Joseph, Jon Tribble, Rodney Jones, M. Brett Gaffney, Maggie Graber, Austin Kodra, Zach Macholz, Josh Bontrager, Ruth Awad, Leslie Brower, Andrew McSorley, Bryan Estes, Max Schleicher, Andrea Wagner, Jonathan Travelstead, Laura Ruffino, Phil Martin, Lucien Darjeun Meadows, Robert Parrott, and Emily Rose Cole.

At the University of South Dakota: Lee Ann Roripaugh, Sara Henning, Teri Kramer, Joshua Rudnik, Kevin Phillips, Grant Riedel, Cheyenne Marco, Russell Shaffer, and Rosie Ahmed.

At Kentucky State University: Karah Stokes, April Fallon, and Richard Taylor.

At the Appalachian Writers Workshop: George Ella Lyon, Maurice Manning, Cathy Smith Bowers, and Diane Gilliam.

At the Kentucky Women Writers Conference: Kim Addonizio and Ada Limón.

At the Mountain Heritage Literary Festival: Aaron Smith.

At FAWC's 24 Pearl Street: Ada Limón and Nancy K. Pearson.

At the Indiana University Writers Conference: Patrick Rosal.

At the Vermont Studio Center: Brian Teare and Edward Hirsch.

For my Kentucky writing friends: Savannah Sipple, Jay McCoy, Keith Stewart, Katerina Stoykova-Klemer, Kimberly Miller, Katie Riley, Bianca Lynne Spriggs, Mark Kinnaird, Michelle Knickerbocker, Linda McAuliffe, Linda Arnold, Jane McCord, Doris Thurber, Sally Wilson, Susan Duvall White, Evelyn Claffy, and Normandi Ellis.

To Heidi Czerwiec, Jennifer Jackson Berry, Claudia Cortese, Barbara Duffey, and Rachel McKibbens for their friendship and help on individual poems and on this manuscript.

Finally, a million thanks to Diane Goettel for calling me to let me know she had accepted my manuscript and was making a long-held dream of mine come true.